THE MYSTIC FLOWERY LAND

Charles JH Halcombe was born in 1865. He left England for Australia at 15 and spent some time as a merchant sailor. He was shipwrecked twice and lived through a mutiny on one of his ships. He spent some time in South Africa from where he departed for Shanghai in 1887, arriving at just 22 years of age. He was to spend the next seven years in China. He appears to have worked for the major British-owned Shanghai English-language newspaper, the *North-China Daily News*, before joining the Imperial Maritime Customs Service as a Watcher.

Halcombe remained with the Customs Service for some years. He resigned in 1893 when stationed at Kiungchow, on the then-remote Hainan Island. Unusually, though not uniquely, Halcombe married a Chinese woman, Liang Ah Ghan, the daughter of a Chefoo merchant.

Paul French, who has introduced and annotated this reprint, was born in London and lived in Shanghai for many years. His book *Midnight in Peking* was a *New York Times* bestseller and a BBC Radio 4 Book of the Week.

Also by Paul French:

Destination Macao

Her Lotus Year

Destination Peking

Strangers on the Praia

Destination Shanghai

City of Devils: A Shanghai Noir

Midnight in Peking: How the Murder of a Young Englishwoman Haunted the Last Days of Old Peking

The Badlands: Decadent Playground of Old Peking

Bloody Saturday: Shanghai's Darkest Day

Supreme Leader: The Making of Kim Jong-un

Betrayal in Paris: How the Treaty of Versailles Led to China's Long Revolution

The Old Shanghai A-Z

Through the Looking Glass: China's Foreign Journalists from Opium Wars to Mao

Carl Crow – A Tough Old China Hand: The Life, Times, and Adventures of an American in Shanghai

North Korea Paranoid Peninsula – A Modern History

The Mystic Flowery Land

A Curious Imperial Maritime Customs Officer's Roamings in Hong Kong and Canton in Southern China's Plague Year

By Charles JH Halcombe

(1896)

Annotated by Paul French

BLACKSMITH BOOKS

China Revisited: No. 5 of a series

The Mystic Flowery Land

ISBN 978-988-76749-8-6

Published by Blacksmith Books
Unit 26, 19/F, Block B, Wah Lok Industrial Centre,
37-41 Shan Mei Street, Fo Tan, Hong Kong
Tel: (+852) 2877 7899
www.blacksmithbooks.com

Cover photograph by Lai Fong (Afong Studio).
Image courtesy of Special Collections, University of Bristol Library (www.hpcbristol.net). Many thanks to Jamie Carstairs and Robert Bickers of the Historical Photographs of China project at the University of Bristol.

CONTENTS

ABOUT CHINA REVISITED

China Revisited is a series of extracted reprints of mid-nineteenth to early-twentieth century Western impressions of Hong Kong, Macao and China. The series comprises excerpts from travelogues or memoirs written by missionaries, diplomats, military personnel, journalists, tourists and temporary sojourners. They came to China from Europe or the United States, some to work or to serve the interests of their country, others out of curiosity. Each excerpt is fully annotated to best provide relevant explications of Hong Kong, Macao and China at the time, to illuminate encounters with historically interesting characters or notable events.

Given the prejudices of the era, what are we to take from these works? Some have a stated agenda, namely colonial control and administration of Hong Kong and Macao, or else proselytising and saving souls for the Christian religion. This is generally obvious in the writing. Others have no stated objective but impressions of the regions, their peoples, and cultures are products of their time and value systems. There is an unsurprising tendency to exoticize, make generally unfavourable comparisons to their home cultures and societies, and to misunderstand what they are witnessing.

They are – whether from American or European sources – invariably from men and women of some formal education. Their acquaintances are among the colonial authorities and foreign diplomats. These "filters" mean that invariably we are given an elite view of China; this is not the experience of the non-officer class sailor, merchant seaman, regular soldier, or working-class visitor. Even before we get to racial prejudice we are encountering class prejudice.

The writers in this series were all men and women of their time, encountering China at specific times in its history. Most of them were visitors or residents for a limited amount of time. However, some, notably the missionaries, did remain for longer – decades in some cases. In general the only foreigners who had credible local language skills were the missionaries, or British colonial district officers and their Portuguese equivalents in Macao, along with some diplomat-scholars. Assumptions were made, prejudices voiced, yet all of these writings have something to reveal of the encounters from which they derived.

FOREWORD

Halcombe's 'Personal Narrative'

This book is an abridged version of Charles JH Halcombe's *The Mystic Flowery Land: A Personal Narrative of a Visit to China* published in 1896 in London by Luzac & Co. of Great Russell Street who specialised in Oriental and foreign books and were the official publishers to the India Office. Luzac had begun as a publisher in the Netherlands before moving to London and maintained printing facilities in Amsterdam. They also published the annual *Luzac's Oriental List and Book Review.*

The Mystic Flowery Land was one of the three major works written by Halcombe that were set in China. In chronological order they were *Called Out; or, The Chung Wang's Daughter, an Anglo-Chinese Romance* (1894); *The Mystic Flowery Land* (1896) and, written after he had returned to England, *Children of Far Cathay: A Social and Political Novel* (1906) published by the *Hongkong Daily Press* and taking a very strong pro-Sun Yat-sen and republican movement position (indeed Halcombe, from his home in Kent, was a member of the China Reform Party). Halcombe published a further novel in 1899, a tale of reincarnation and ancient Rome, *The Love of a Former Life*, which received unenthusiastic reviews.

Though his memoir was published in 1896 and was written in England in 1894 and 1895, Halcombe is referring to his earlier experiences in China, mostly from around 1887 beginning with his initial arrival in China at Shanghai. In these excerpts he is recalling events in Hong Kong and Canton in the early half of the 1890s. We know this from certain clues. For instance, he notes the colony's Public Works Department, which was established in 1891. Additionally, he refers to landing at Pedder's Wharf, though this was demolished in January 1894. These two references place Halcombe in Hong Kong in 1892 and 1893, while his detailed description of the bubonic plague outbreak places him there again in 1894.

The book contains a number of photographs and illustrations though no specific credits are provided and so we cannot be sure who took these images.

The Mystic Flowery Land is dedicated by Halcombe to:

MY NUMEROUS EUROPEAN AND CHINESE FRIENDS IN THE IMPERIAL MARITIME CUSTOMS SERVICE

AND ABOARD
THE COASTING STEAMERS IN CHINA
THIS WORK IS MOST AFFECTIONATELY
DEDICATED IN REMEMBRANCE
OF MANY BYGONE HAPPY DAYS SPENT IN
THEIR COMPANY.

INTRODUCTION

'I landed in Hongkong in the evening when all was brightly lit up by electric light; and if the reader will, in imagination, accompany me on a ramble through the city, I shall be most happy to traverse the distance again as his guide.'

Charles JH Halcombe was born in 1865, the grandson of a barrister and Member of Parliament (MP) for Dover in Kent, and the son of a civil servant. He left England for Australia at 15 and spent some time as a merchant sailor. He was shipwrecked twice – in December 1881 off the French coast, and in January 1883 off Cape Horn – and also lived through a mutiny on board one of his ships. He spent some time in South Africa from where he departed for Shanghai in 1887 arriving in May of that year at just 22 years of age.[1] He

1 Halcombe recalled his time in South Africa in *Travels in the Transvaal: True, Instructure, and Adventurous (including Cape Life: As It Was)* in a short pamphlet published in 1899 in Holland, initially in Dutch and then translated into English.

was to spend the next seven years in China. He appears to have worked for approximately a year for the major British-owned Shanghai English-language newspaper, the *North-China Daily News*, before joining the Imperial Maritime Customs Service as a Watcher.

Halcombe remained with the Imperial Maritime Customs Service for some years, gaining a promotion to Second Class Tidewaiter (a customs officer who boards ships on their arrival to enforce customs regulations). He resigned in 1893 when stationed at Kiungchow (Qiongzhou), on the then fairly remote Hainan Island. It appears that Halcombe had long harboured thoughts of becoming a published author, hence his early stint on the *North-China Daily News* and that he had also apparently been working on a novel and some poems while a customs officer.

Unusually, though not uniquely, Halcombe married a Chinese woman, Liang Ah Ghan, the daughter of a Chefoo (Yantai) merchant of the author's acquaintance. Halcombe was apparently visiting Liang Ah Ghan's father in 1888-1889 when rebels threatened to attack the house and kill the foreigner inside. Halcombe claims Liang Ah Ghan (who was often called Nina in English) spirited him away to safety dressed in a disguise of Chinese robes. From this encounter, romance blossomed and they married in 1892. This tale of their meeting and romance (which may or may not be completely true) excited some interest when *The Mystic Flowery Land* was published, with various newspapers noting that it would include (as indeed it does) a photographic portrait of the author 'with his wife in her Oriental costume'.[2] *The Glasgow Herald* suggested that Halcombe could provide especially interesting insights into China due to his 'Chinese bride'.[3]

Halcombe, with Liang Ah Ghan, returned to England in late 1894, presumably fleeing the bubonic plague outbreak in Hong Kong and southern China at the time. The couple lived in Herne Bay and Dover. Halcombe was active in the English branch of Sun Yat-sen's China Reform Party and wrote to the newspapers on several occasions supporting China's republican revolution of 1911. In the First World War, Halcombe was in charge of the records office at Dover Castle. He continued to live in Kent into the 1920s, becoming a member of the Herne Bay Urban District Council and was also involved in the local amateur-dramatics society.

Halcombe died in 1931 at his home in Dover, leaving Liang Ah Ghan a widow. The couple had no children. The historian Robert Bickers notes that Liang Ah Ghan/Nina was baptised in a Herne Bay church. Liang Ah Ghan died

---

2 *The Belfast News*, November 23, 1896, p.7.

3 *The Glasgow Herald*, December 24, 1896, p.8.

in 1949 in Folkestone, though sadly little to nothing is known of her life in England.

***

What does Halcombe tell us of interest about Hong Kong and Canton in *The Mystic Flowery Land*? Well, nothing if you believe the books reviewer of the *Birmingham Daily Gazette* – 'His ramble through Hong Kong is a poor and scrappy bit of work with evidence of haste and only superficial knowledge.'[4] However, *The Glasgow Herald* (in the same review that made much of Halcombe's insider knowledge due to his having a Chinese wife) considered the book 'worth recommending even to those who have read a great deal about China.'[5]

After arriving at the long-gone Pedder's Wharf by sampan and checking into the imposing Hongkong Hotel (noting the, to Halcombe, high numbers of Portuguese in the area), Halcombe does take an extended literary stroll along Queen's Road, inviting the reader to join him. He notes the colonial architecture as well as Sikh and well-armed Chinese policemen and the Hongkong and Shanghai Bank (before its demolition in the 1930s).

But what Halcombe concentrates on is the western end of Queen's Road, beyond the barracks and cricket

---

4 *Birmingham Daily Gazette*, September 21, 1898, p.8.

5 *The Glasgow Herald*, December 24, 1896, p.8.

ground. Here Halcombe finds the "rum-mills" and Chinese theatres, the Sing-Song girls and gamblers.

Halcombe is also interested in the lives and fortunes of various "beach combers", those rather indigent Europeans who through choice or bad luck have washed up in Hong Kong and along the China coast and are down on their luck. His story of Marshall – actually a Shanghai tale – is illuminating of what happened to those who fell through the cracks of China coast life, succumbed to alcohol or narcotics or just plain bankruptcy or ill health.

Halcombe's descriptions of Canton begin with arriving by coastal steamer and the route from Hong Kong to the city. As a Maritime Customs man Halcombe had an affinity for those engaged in seafaring or the riverine life in China and so is generous in his details of this world, from the infamous Flower Boats to the working river steamers. He is also keen on temples (including Canton's major mosque) and Chinese gods and describes these – many at the time in a state of some disrepair and neglect – in detail. This interest in temples extends to Halcombe's detailed description of Hong Kong Island's Man Mo Temple, still a well-known and well-utilised institution on Hollywood Road.

But it is perhaps Halcombe's description of the terrible bubonic plague that hit Hong Kong in 1894 that stands out to the reader today – so recently in the wake of SARS and Covid-19. Hong Kong in that plague year resembles at times a city under zombie attack – he recalls '…in very virulent cases I have seen men suddenly struck down in the street. The victim would stagger, like a drunken man, and fall – gasping for breath, and foaming at the mouth; and would frequently die before the hospital could be reached.'

Plagues came and went in Hong Kong, again in 1895 and occasionally until 1929, killing thousands. But the 1894 plague was the worst in terms of spread, failed efforts at containment and deaths. In hindsight we can see it as a major turning point in the history of colonial Hong Kong, forcing the government to re-examine its policy towards the Chinese community, and invest in the wellbeing of the Chinese in terms of slum clearance, clean water and medical care. Halcombe could not, at the time of his writing, know that this would be a result but it's an outcome he repeatedly suggests should happen and fervently hopes for.

From a photograph by J. Craik, Herne-Bay.

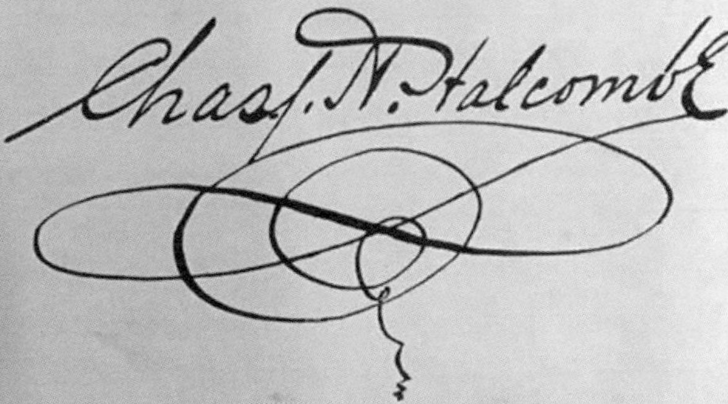

A RAMBLE IN HONG KONG

(This text and spellings taken from *The Mystic Flowery Land: A Personal Narrative*, Chapter XXIV, XXV, by Charles JH Halcombe, London, Luzac & Co. (Publishers to the India Office), first British edition, 1896).

HONGKONG, or "Fragrant Streams", lies between 22° 9', 22° 1', North Latitude, and 114° 5', 115° 18' East Longitude, and is one of several islands situated near the South-Eastern coast of China, and at the mouth of the Pearl River – eighty-two miles south-west of Canton, and thirty-seven miles east of Macao, with a length of about ten miles and a breadth of from three to four miles – its area being thirty square miles.

It is the emporium of British Trade with China, and the distribution centre of Far Eastern commerce; its principal imports being opium, flour, sugar, oil, earthenware, woollen and cotton goods, sandalwood (the latter coming from Western Australia), vegetables, grain and livestock.

The transaction of the silk and tea trades in South China are also chiefly controlled by firms in Hongkong.[6]

During the hostilities in 1840 and 41 *which ensued from the action of the Chinese authorities at Canton to suppress the Opium Trade*, the harbour of Hongkong was used by the British fleet and its transports.[7] The island was partially ceded to Great Britain in a convention entered into between Captain Elliot R.N. and the Chinese General, Ki Shan, in 1841.[8]

---

6 Spellings of Hong Kong as alternatively Hongkong were common up until the early 1950s.

7 Halcombe's italics.

8 R.N. = Royal Navy. Halcombe is referring to the Treaty of Chuanpei, or the Chuenpi Convention, that formalised the ceding of Hong Kong to the British and preceded the better-known Treaty of Nanking in 1842. Ki Shan, or more often at the time Ki Shen, is Qishan (1785-1854), a Mongol noble and Qing Dynasty official. He negotiated with the British without seeking approval from the Qing imperial court which enraged the Daoguang Emperor. Qishan was arrested, taken under arms to Peking, and his property confiscated before he was sentenced to military service. He was pardoned and reinstated in 1842 and posted to Tibet and Sichuan. He later oversaw the Qing forces opposing the Taiping Rebellion. He died in an army camp during the campaign to suppress the Taiping. Charles Elliot (1801-1875) was first administrator of Hong Kong and Plenipotentiary and Chief Superintendent of British Trade in China in 1841 and a key founder in the establishment of Hong Kong as a British colony.

After the resumption of hostilities, a treaty was signed at Nankin, in 1842, in which Hongkong was declared as fully relinquished to the British; and on April 5th of 1843 was erected into the full status of a Crown Colony by an Order in Council. The official occasion of taking possession of the island is mentioned by Sir Edward Belcher, in his "Voyage of H.M.S. Sulpher", thus: -

"We landed on Monday night the 25th of January 1841, at fifteen minutes past eight a.m., and being the *bona fide* possessors, Her Majesty's health was drunk with three cheers on Possession Mount. On the 26th the squadron arrived; the marines were landed, the Union Jack hoisted on our post, and formal possession taken of the island by Commodore Sir J.G. Bremer, accompanied by the other officers of the squadron, under a *feu-de-joie* from the marines and the Royal Salute from the ships of war.[9] On the Kowloon peninsula were situated two batteries, which might have commanded the anchorage, but which appeared to be but thinly manned; these

9 *Feu de joie* (French: fire of joy) is a form of formal celebratory gunfire consisting of a celebratory rifle salute. James Gordon Bremer (1786-1850) was a Royal Navy officer in the Napoleonic Wars, the First Anglo-Burmese War (1824-1826) and served as temporary commander-in-chief of British forces in the First Opium War (1839-1842).

received due notice to withdraw their men and guns, as agreed by the late treaty."[10]

The colony presents a very picturesque and imposing appearance on entering the harbour – the background tawny green mountains, and the white-coloured European residences rising in terraces, one above the other, on its steep slopes. Of an evening the effect is remarkably magnificent – when all the lights of these houses glimmer and twinkle, illumining with myriads of bright stars, like fairy lamps, the dark mountain side, up which they creep – growing gradually lesser and smaller – until the beacon-crowned summit is reached.

I landed in Hongkong in the evening when all was brightly lit up by electric light; and if the reader will, in imagination, accompany me on a ramble through the city, I shall be most happy to traverse the distance again as his guide.

We go ashore from the steamer in a long and somewhat narrow sailing *sampan*, commanded by an old Chinese

---

10 Admiral Sir Edward Belcher (1799-1877), British naval officer and hydrographer. On January 25, 1841, Belcher landed on Possession Point at the north shore of Hong Kong Island and made the first British survey of Hong Kong's harbour. Halcombe is quoting from *The Zoology of the Voyage of H.M.S. Sulphur, Under the Command of Captain Sir Edward Belcher During the Years 1836-42*, published under the authority of the Lords Commissioners of the Admiralty (1843-1846).

woman who steers the craft, and manned by her children who were taught to pull an oar and handle the sails almost from the day of their birth. For they are bred and brought up aboard the *sampan* which is a family heirloom – and there they pass all the days of their life, twice a day going ashore to the market.

On landing at Pedder's Wharf, we are surrounded by chair and ricksha coolies whom we gently disperse with a few judiciously bestowed raps from our sticks, and are allowed to pass forward across the Bund which is faced by rows of tall buildings, more roomy and comfortable than of architectural beauty.[11] These are the offices of the wealthy mercantile firms whose steamers plough the Eastern seas from the Gulf of Pechili to the Tonquin Gulf.[12] But these offices are closed at this hour, as the *hong* men – or taipans as the Chinese call them – go home at 4 p.m.: many of them living over the water on the mainland at Kowloon. Between there and Hongkong, lines of smart passenger launches run continually. Other

---

11 Pedder's Wharf was built originally in 1841, though the wharf Halcombe would have landed at was a second construction completed in 1886 at the junction of Pedder Street and Des Voeux Road. It was a simple platform extending from the Praya wall with six sets of steps leading down to the water. It was demolished in 1894.

12 Gulf of Pechili = Bohai Sea; Tonquin Gulf = Gulf of Tonkin.

residents, especially during the hot summer months, reside upon the Peak which is reached by an almost perpendicular tramway constructed by Mr. Bowdler, an eminent and skilled engineer who is now supervising and controlling, as Engineer-in-Chief, the important and difficult work of reclaiming, filling in and draining a large portion of the harbour; the reclaimed ground being divided into building lots, which will greatly add to the imposing appearance of the colony.[13] I have unfortunately mislaid my last interesting letter from this highly respected, and eminently clever gentleman, or I should take the liberty of quoting a portion to show the gigantic proportions of the work he is carrying out. A large part of the Western section of Hongkong has lately been redrained under the supervision of Mr. Bidgood, Foreman Engineer of the Public Works Department of whom – like his hard-working chief – the Colony may well be proud, for a more trustworthy and zealous servant could hardly be found.[14] On one occasion, during a heavy

---

13 Edward Bowdler (1831-1907) arrived in Hong Kong in 1874 from a previous posting in Mauritius. Served as Assistant Surveyor General of Hong Kong for 24 years, overseeing various projects including the construction of the Hong Kong Observatory as well as significant reclamation works. Additionally Bowdler was a Member of the Executive and the Legislative Council from 1893.

14 The Public Works Department was founded in 1891.

typhoon and at the imminent risk of losing his life, he descended at midnight into one of the large drains under repair which had not been properly shored up by the Chinese contractor and in consequence endangered some buildings which threatened to fall at any moment. For hours during the worst of the storm and with a rushing torrent around him he nobly worked there – thus saving many lives and much valuable property.

The clock in the Bell Tower facing us, with its illuminated dial, now strikes eight as we enter the Hongkong Hotel for the purpose of booking rooms.[15] What an immense place it is! and how lofty. Apartments here cost a trifle – six dollars per diem – a trifle more than one can generally afford for any length of time. These elaborate pillars, panels, traceries, and statues mean weighty capital heavily sunk.

"This way, sars – loom hundred-forty – look out – get in, sars – *haiya*!"

A polite celestial indeed! He nearly took my breath away when he shoved us on this concern, and we started for the roof. I don't like these lifts – too much of a hurry

---

15 The Hongkong Hotel opened in 1868 at the junction of Queen's Road and Pedder Street and was owned by the Hongkong Hotel Company (later Hongkong and Shanghai Hotels Ltd). The Bell Tower Halcombe is referring to is the Clock Tower that stood on Queen's Road, built in 1863 and demolished in 1913.

altogether for the Far East. These rooms are comfortable enough, though – and so they ought to be. We will take a stroll by moonlight – by electric light, I should say, for the streets are simply flooded with the weird illuminant which plays on a panorama of stately abodes and *hongs* of merchant princes. These lofty and inaccessible-looking buildings seem to have quite trampled to dust the homelier looking shanties of the earlier sailing-ship days. What a busy crowd, too, ever moves along! Velvet-lined chairs with starred and striped bearers, fair ladies; old men walking, young swells riding, and men-of-war sailors rattling recklessly along in rickshas; and dirty vagrants selling the sweetest flowers from Canton.

"Wantchee button-hole, Sir?"

"No thanks – can't afford such adornments." There is very little money about the colony just at present – it has all gone in the bogus companies, flying lots, and "salted" gold and silver mines. That is why everybody you meet looks so anxious – very different form the old prosperous days when the financial foundations of these halls were laid.

Why the place seems over-run with Portuguese! They almost crowd one off the pavement. It is about time a stop was put to this wholesale emigration from Macao. But I suppose it is no use bringing new laws into force – Macao must be empty – left with its one half-forgotten redeeming point – the statue of Camoens who wrote his "Lusciad" there.[16] They have left that city, vulgarly speaking, "bottom up" – and have taken a "hand", or "chipped in" as I heard someone remark, to gamble this city away – to reduce it to its primeval state of "granite stones, empty bottles and cigar ends."[17]

The thoroughfares are certainly most creditably kept, one doesn't have to tuck his dress-trousers into sea-boots now or walk and tumble over plank bridges. We won't trouble about climbing up and down the hilly tiers of streets tonight – we may as well keep straight along the

---

16 Halcombe obviously means the Portuguese poet Luís Vaz de Camões, often spelt "Camoens" in English, who resided in Macao between 1562 and 1565 as Superintendent for the Dead and Missing and wrote at least part of his epic poem *Os Lusíadas*, or *The Lusiads*, while in the Portuguese colony.

17 Halcombe's prejudices against the Portuguese were not uncommon of the British in Hong Kong at the time. The British colony had certainly rapidly eclipsed the Portuguese colony in terms of economic opportunity. However, while many Portuguese/Macanese moved to Hong Kong they invariably played valuable roles filling positions from the 1840s as Hong Kong bureaucrats, traders' and bank clerks, printers, typesetters, teachers and newspapermen. Already by the early 1850s a total of 322 Portuguese men and 137 women had relocated to Hong Kong. Despite discrimination from the British, they mostly stayed. By 1897 more than half of Hong Kong's Portuguese population of around 2,500 had been born in the British colony.

Queen's Road – which is the Regent Street of the Orient – on a smooth easterly course which leads to "Happy Valley" where the Europeans are buried in a beautiful garden of tombs and flowers. There is not much fear of being robbed when those great strapping British, and tall fierce looking Sikhs and keen if somewhat diminutive Chinese policemen – some carrying carbines, cutlasses and revolvers, are patrolling this broad well-lighted road.

The Chinese police, or *lukongs* are much feared by the poorer class of native inhabitants from whom they frequently contrive to extort money.[18] The unnecessary and uncalled-for brutality of the general *lukong* has long been known and patiently tolerated by the poor and comparatively helpless class of Chinese itinerant hawkers – especially the sugar-cane vendors. A striking instance of this kind was brought to my notice one evening, when a poor wretched looking coolie, probably with a wife and family dependent on his small earnings, had placed his little portable stall at the side of the road in D'Aguilar Street. He was trying to sell a few pieces of sugar-cane when suddenly a *lukong* came along, upset the contents of the stall in the road, and for some minutes indulged in a little of what he thought sport by dragging the unfortunate

18 *Lukong* (Cantonese: *lougung*), a term for an ethnic Chinese police constable.

proprietor about by the *queue*, and then hustling him off to the police station.

Now we pass the magnificent building occupied by the Hongkong and Shanghai Bank, with its lofty domed-roof, the ceiling of which is a pale azure colour with golden stars.[19] Further on stands a large fountain and the splendidly constructed buildings comprising the Chamber of Commerce, Museum and theatre of which Hongkong may be justly proud. Now we are beginning to enter old Hongkong, the familiar tree-shaded parts beyond which are the barracks. On our left is the well-kept cricket ground – in old times the Public Recreation Ground.

We pause here a while, leaning against the palings – and listen to the excellent band of the Shropshire Regiment playing across the way there at the officers' mess.[20] Someone might confer a great boon on the public by placing a few seats at convenient and unobtrusive spots – say under the trees on the east side of Murray Road, or somewhere in this vicinity, as numbers of residents

---

19 Halcombe is referring to the second HSBC building in Hong Kong, on Queen's Road and completed in 1886. It had a noted octagonal dome. The building was demolished in 1934.

20 Palings = fencing made from long, thin pieces of wood.

come here in the pleasant summer evenings to hear the music.[21]

There must be something peculiarly attractive about this little Far Eastern colony. For I have noticed that after a man has lived here a few years, although he may then leave, and be absent perhaps for almost a lifetime – he generally comes back again sooner or later and settles down for the rest of his days.

The band stops playing at nine o'clock, so now we will retrace our steps, repass the hotel, and take a walk along the more lively western part of the settlement. How cool and refreshing this night breeze is! – Better to hear the reposeful rustling of the tall trees overhead than the rumbling of the cabs, trams and trains ever heard in western lands. How quiet it is becoming – just the time for a walk – the very time to view Hongkong peacefully nestling under the shadow of those majestic hills whence the lights glimmer like meteors, so high are the houses above us.

---

21 Murray Road was named after Sir George Murray (1772-1846), a soldier and politician from Scotland. He never seems to have visited Hong Kong so the honour was probably due to his stint as Master-General of the Ordnance for the British Army at the time of the road's construction. Murray House, Murray Building and Murray Barracks were also all named after him.

As we enter the western half of Queen's Road, which runs parallel with the harbour frontage, the shops become almost exclusively Chinese, and the quaint signboards and paper lanterns begin to show themselves. Here and there are "rum-mills" whence the sound of loud and discordant music and the bustling and clatter of feet proceed – evidently to the entire satisfaction of poor Jack ashore who is there gracefully fleeced of his hard-earned pay to the tune of fantastic music.[22]

Now we come to a Chinese theatre – the celebrated Know Shing Theatre into which numbers of smiling-faced sons of Han and their comely ladies are crowding.[23] We may as well enter with them. On the left-hand side of the doorway is the ticket office enclosed by wooden bars and wire lattice-work. Seats in the gallery, part of which is reserved for ladies, cost from 50 cents to $1, and those in the lower part or body of the theatre from 10 to 25 cents. You pay your money, receive a red ticket, and pass into the well-filled house. You can sit where you like – on the back of a seat if it suits you, and everybody is agreeable. Some prefer to go and sit on stage near the actors. The building is square shaped – somewhat resembling a chapel, with the galleries on either side and facing the stage which

---

22 Jack ashore – a drunken sailor

23 Halcombe means the Ko Shing Theatre, built around 1890 at 117 Queen's Road West. It was demolished in 1973.

occupies the same position as ours but has no curtain of scenery – these are quite unknown in a Chinese theatre. City walls, mountains, temples, palaces, fortifications, furniture and other objects are represented by chairs while many of the scenes are delineated by pantomimic attitudes and motions.

As my learned friend, Mr. Stanton, of Hongkong writes:- "Their scenery is inferior to what ours was, at the Cockpit and Globe theatres in Shakespeare's time, and about equal to Peter Quince's scenery in his 'most lamentable comedy and most cruel death of Pyramus and Thisby,' as shown in the 'Midsummer Night's Dream', where a man with loam over him represents a wall and his spread open fingers a cranny for lovers to whisper through. The orchestra, which through the ear-splitting nature of its music, is the great hindrance to foreigners enjoying a play, occupies the rear-central part of the stage between the doorways leading to the green-room. This green-room is an interesting place, full of strange things and stranger looking people, of arms, and armour of every period of Chinese history except the last 200 years, of hideous masks, and beards of various colours, of richly embroidered robes and patched rags, and so on.

"One dirty looking fellow dons imperial robes and flowing beard and struts the stage a full-blown Emperor, another slips on embroidered robes and long moustache and is transformed into a sapient Minister of State, another daubs his cheeks with paint, puts on a coiffure, a lady's dress and tiny shoes and totters about a golden-lilied princess; and so on with all the rest – gods, genii, heroes and villains.[24] They make up very cleverly, especially the men who impersonate females."[25]

A few of the leading lights of the Chinese stage received salaries ranging from 5,000 to 9,000 dollars per annum, and the lesser ones from 600 to 1,200 dollars a year. But their life is not altogether a very enviable one; and most of them are confirmed opium smokers. Unlike our actors they are looked down upon and despised, and can never rise to any position, however clever they may be.[26]

---

24 'Golden-lilied' indicating bound feet.

25 Mr Stanton is Vincent John Stanton (1817-1891), an English missionary with the Church Missionary Society to Hong Kong. Stanton was the first colonial chaplain of Hong Kong and was involved in the foundation of both St. John's Cathedral and St. Paul's College in the colony. His attempt to trivialise Chinese theatre by a like-for-like comparison with the conventions of the English Elizabethan theatre is strange and somewhat pointless. Quince, Pyramus and Thisby are all characters in Shakespeare's *A Midsummer Night's Dream* (c.1596).

26 Halcombe may be somewhat exaggerating the position of British actors, and especially actresses, in the late nineteenth century.

At half past eleven we come out of the theatre, after spending a couple of hours most enjoyably in the battles and love scenes of some bygone dynasty. Now we will return home.

What a transformation Queen's Road has undergone within an hour or two! Before, all was bustle – now, all is silent and quiet, save for the occasional regulation thief-warning tramp of a policeman or the voice of a chair or ricksha coolie soliciting a fare. But hark – what is that sharp note, as of a castanet? That sound somehow seems familiar to me. Ah, yes – poor creatures, here they come. A young girl – a "sing-song" girl, walking hand-in-hand and chatting pleasantly with an aged woman. Both are blind – the blind leading the blind; but the poor creatures seem happy – happier indeed and more contented than most of their sex you meet. Hongkong by night would not be complete without its poor blind nightingales.

Hullo! What's that bell ringing for? I thought so – here they come dashing along. FIRE! fire! stand aside please. All right constable – good night. We are not in for this sport – we shall see it all and a great deal more in tomorrow's newspapers. There goes a poor reporter for copy – buttoning his clothes over his pyjamas.

One night, when a great conflagration was in full blaze, and the shore and floating engines were all in use, an event occurred which was nearly the cause of another fire, perhaps of a worse nature. A sergeant of the police on entering a Chinese house to seize some opium, about when he had evidently got information, found congregated there a large party of gamblers who, in their desperate hurry to escape, knocked over two kerosene lamps, leaving the sergeant to fight the flames which he accomplished successfully in place of arresting the gang of rascals.

AN INTERESTING CASE

(This section originally appeared as a letter in the *Hongkong Daily Press*)[27]

Few people, not even our zealous missionaries, who dwell in the central quarter of Hongkong, especially the wealthier portions of the community, know or have any adequate idea how some of the poorer people inhabiting the outlying districts east and west of them live or, more properly speaking, manage to exist – which is very often a puzzle to themselves; or what sport of people they are who do actually exist there. No doubt some imagine they know all about it, others make a few half-hearted inquiries, while the large majority rarely condescend to give this distasteful subject a thought; and if the thought comes,

27 The *Hongkong Daily Press* was founded in 1857 and closed around 1937. Founded and edited by George M Ryder, it claimed to be the first daily newspaper in Hong Kong. At times the paper was highly critical of the colonial administration, and one of its editors was imprisoned on a charge of libel. Its offices were at the junction of Wyndham Street and Glenealy in Central.

they ignominiously dispel it as bearing no affinity to their business. Most of the residents know where the Jewish fraternity all herd together in good old Mesopotamian style – clustering about their headman; and where the Parsees, Mohamedans, and Armenians live happily on first floors, using the ground floors for opium godowns, while they eternally upend the "Almighty Dollar."[28] We all know about these worthy people, except their own business, which, unlike most men, they mind themselves. The Chinese live all about the European residents, and we pretend to know all about their funny little ways, and characteristics, and even write about them. While "John's" wee ferret eyes unceasingly blink – for he knows we know nothing at all – at least nothing of any importance.[29]

I do not say that Hongkong is the only place where this uncharitable ignorance exists, for even Shanghai with all its philanthropists and charitable institutions, and its well endowed missions, is exactly the same – if not more ignorant in this respect. As an instance of this, I will, before proceeding further, open the eyes of some by relating a sad event which took place in Shanghai some

---

28 Halcombe is, in a rather ham-fisted and prejudicial way, referring to the Baghdadi Jewish community. A godown being a storehouse/warehouse.

29 Halcombe is referring to "John Chinaman", a stock caricature of the Chinese labouring man in the nineteenth century in European and American newspapers.

six or seven years ago. There was one general reporter, on the staff of a well-known journal there named Thomas Marshall, who was of an eminently respectable old English family, his father being, I believe, a colonel in the army. Now Marshall, who was a well-educated and gentlemanly fellow and a smart writer – when he chose to wield the quill – used to suffer from periodic attacks of ebriety, at which times he became very irregular in his habits and failed to adequately perform his duties.[30] So he was discharged; and most people knew, or made it their business to find out, why. Give a dog a bad name and it will stick to him, above all places it will stick fastest in Shanghai. Consequently the unfortunate ex-reporter was unable to obtain any further employment. He had not sufficient money to leave the Settlement – and he was too proud to beg or even to write home.[31] I myself used to frequently see him of a morning going from one *hong* to another along the Bund – on the alert for any vacancy which *might* (but never could) occur for *him*.[32]

After a time I quite lost sight of him, and, concluding that he must have left the Settlement, I thought no

30 Ebriety = drunkenness.

31 Meaning the International Settlement of Shanghai (the combined foreign concessions of 1863, excepting the separate French Concession).

32 The author's italics.

more about him. Months passed away and at length I left Shanghai for the North of China. Some three years afterwards a paragraph in a Shanghai paper caught my eye. It was a brief account of the death of poor Marshall – it was a glaring proof of the injustice that had been done him. It recalled very forcibly to my mind the words of Juvenal:

"Want is the scorn of every wealthy fool,
And wit in rags is turned to ridicule."

His untimely death was indeed a stern reproach to the foreign community of Shanghai, by whom it ought not to be forgotten; and also a stern warning to young men leaving England to take up positions in our eastern colonies.

It appeared from the evidence of a ricksha coolie, his last friend on earth, that the poor fellow had tried everywhere but failed to obtain employment of any kind. He soon ran short of money, and rather than also run into debt – as many would have pardonably done – he quietly moved into a small room, a miserable little hole in a Chinese house in China-town.[33] There he used to write some of his clever articles and essays, most of which were returned to him, with those well-known words "declined with thanks

33 Halcombe means the Chinese-administered Shanghai district of Nanshi or Nantao, commonly known as the Old Town.

and regrets." He never complained to anyone; and when he was seen, he was always dressed respectably and even carefully; and he always smiled and nodded pleasantly to those whom he knew – those who had claimed his friendship when he was in better circumstances. He grew perceptibly thinner, though – thin from want of proper food. The beautiful part of this painful story comes in here.

Poor Marshall was always kind and gentle – of a gentle, sensitive nature; and was friendly and considerate to everybody, even down to his Chinese "boy," who, strange to relate, became really devoted to him. When the master left the staff of the newspaper, the servant followed him and, although he knew that his master had not money to pay him wages, he waited on him and lived with him, and they went down the hill together. The boy also tried to obtain work as both his master and he had not food to eat. He was equally unfortunate. At last he managed to hire a ricksha and turned ricksha-coolie.

Marshall grew weaker and thinner, and latterly was not able to leave the hovel in which they lived – so his maintenance fell entirely upon the faithful "boy" whose small earnings were sometimes hardly sufficient to give them congee – still he managed somehow to pay for the room and give his master some food to eat. But the poor friendless fellow grew weaker and weaker, and at last was not able to eat the rice given him. In this dire extremity he sent a polite letter to one of his countrymen in the Settlement, asking him to kindly send him a plate of soup, as he was very ill and unable to get out. The proud foreigner did not respond or deign to reply to this urgent and final appeal. A few days afterwards – in one of the richest and proudest communities in the world – and on the very doorstep, as it were, of princely merchants, as far as riches are concerned, poor Thomas Marshall died of starvation. The matter was hushed up; and the benevolent foreigners rewarded the ricksha coolie with two hundred dollars and set him up in business; and the verdict returned at the inquest, was that the deceased had died of "general debility – accelerated through want of proper nourishment."

Having narrated this instance, I will now pick up the thread of my discourse where I left it – leaving those who doubt the veracity of my assertions to turn over the files of old Shanghai papers of '88 or '89. Most residents in Hongkong have heard about the proverbial "beachcomber," and know that such beings do actually exist there. How they live, what they are like, whither they come, and how they become what they are, is not of much concern or interest. Many people imagine that every disorderly or oddly dressed and dissipated looking merchant seaman is one of these unfortunate creatures. But they are much mistaken, for the genuine "beachcomber" is very rarely seen – except early in the morning or late in the evening. Even then he generally shuns his fellow men, except when driven by want to ask alms: then he slinks out into one of the larger thoroughfares and keeps along close to the wall, until he sees a person in better circumstances than himself. then he darts to his side and, with head bent, stammers out almost incoherent words, which sound like a muttered prayer or curse. He receives a coin. And is gone – seen no more. The question is, cannot something be done for these poor wretches? I have talked it over with the authorities, consuls and police when I tried to get a man an order to the Sailors Home for a night's lodging, and the only satisfaction I got was "Lock him up as a vagrant – put him in gaol."[34]

Some time ago, during one of my evening rambles through the western district of Hongkong and Taipinshan – the Seven Dials or Ratcliff Highway of China – I saw a strange and awful looking creature, hardly human in appearance, slink out of a dirty alleyway and stand gazing

34 A Sailors' Home was founded in Hong Kong in a hostel building at West Point (off Pok Fu Lam Road and then the northernmost point on the western half of Hong Kong Island) in 1863. It was adjacent to St. Peter's Church (built slightly later) which became known as the Seamen's Church. The Home was superseded in 1910 by the creation of The Missions to Seamen residential seamen's hostel on Johnston Road.

absently up and down the gloomy thoroughfare.[35] I will endeavour to describe his appearance. He was of medium height, with back almost bent into a hunch as he stooped forward with rounded shoulders and bowed head; his hair was matted and so long that it reached below the shoulders in a tangled mess; his face was of a ghastly yellowish-white colour, and his dark eyes sunk into their blueish sockets. He wore an old felt hat with the brim partly worn away, an old battered overcoat covered the filthy rags beneath, and his blistered feet were enclosed in a pair of time-worn dancing-pumps that were tied to his feet with pieces of rag and string.

I stopped before the poor wretch and asked him who he was and where he lived. He stood still, and gazed blankly up and down the street, did not take any notice whatever, and seemed quite oblivious of my presence. After putting further questions and eliciting no reply, I took hold of his arm and shook it. He suddenly raised his head and with a wan smile on his half-daft face, asked what I wanted with

35 Taipinshan = Tai Ping Shan. One of the earliest Chinese settlements in the city that was unfortunately hit by bubonic plague in the late nineteenth century. Halcombe is comparing it to the notorious London rookeries (slum districts prone to disease outbreaks due to overcrowding and unsanitary conditions) of Seven Dials in Covent Garden and the Ratcliff Highway in the East End.

him. I told him I should like to help him if he would only tell me about himself.

"No, no; no help!" was all he said, as he again hung his head. It was with the greatest difficulty that I prevailed on him to articulate a few words, and then I could hardly understand what he said or meant. At last I gave him to understand that I wished him to come to my house next morning. I wrote the address down, and then, as he nodded an assent, left him standing there gazing with an unmeaning smile at the envelope which I had put in his hand.

Next morning at about 10 a.m. I heard an unusual commotion in the street. Thinking it was someone being escorted to the police station, I got up and went on the verandah. Who should I see but the poor wretch I had met the previous night, walking rapidly along the centre of the street followed by hundreds of yelling Chinese. He seemed to take no notice of them whatever; but – with back hunched, and head bowed – came doggedly along, straight to the house and entered the front-door. Inviting him into the kitchen, I asked him to sit down. I then managed after a time, with the assistance of my wife, to make him speak. I learned that he was a French-American born in California; that he came out to China a year back, as second cook of the steamer *Gaelic* from San Francisco; that he had tried to obtain work and had failed, that he had tried to leave Hongkong, but was unable; that for months he had not shown himself in the day time, being ashamed of his wild appearance, having no money to improve it, and no friends; that he slept anywhere and very often in the woods on the sides of the hills, and lastly that his name was Sams – and that he very much wished to obtain employment as cook or watchman anywhere.[36]

I took him out and at last got a barber to cut his year's growth of hair; and then I sent him to have a bath, and finally rigged him up in a clean suit of flannel clothes, boots and hat. And lo – he was another being! I hardly knew him as the same man. I then gave him a good meal, and, when he was satisfied, talked seriously and sensibly to him. When he left my house, he carried himself erect, created no sensation and looked respectable, infinitely more so than many; and that blank imbecilic look had faded from his face. I took him to the Central Police Station to make inquiries about him. None of the Europeans there had ever seen him before, and his reputation was clean. Then I sent him with a letter to the American Consul, who politely informed me that he was unable to help the man; the master of the Sailors' Home said the same; and in spite of my earnest entreaties, nothing was

---

36 *RMS Gaelic* was a passenger and cargo liner built for the White Star Line chartered to the Occidental and Oriental Steamship Company (the O&O) for service in the Far East.

done for him.[37] I endeavoured to obtain a berth for him aboard the American ship *Martha Davis*, but was equally unsuccessful.[38]

Shortly afterwards, on making inquiries about this unfortunate man, I found out that since he had dressed decently and had been presentable enough to appear in the streets and, as I advised look for employment, he had been pounced upon by the police and imprisoned as a vagrant because he had no "visible means of support" or some other equally plausible excuse. How can these poor outcasts better their position when no one will give them work, and there is no institution provided for them? They must either hide away in any filthy den or venture out and be captured and imprisoned amongst criminals – and treated like dogs rather than human beings, simply because they have no money, no home, and no friends. If a man commits the error of running away from his ship – which is perhaps a floating hell – is he to be deprived of again returning to his native land and of living respectably amongst his fellow men? I have seen so much of the miseries of these so-called "beachcombers" that I consider

---

37 Halcombe does not date this story precisely and so could be referring either to R.E. Withens, Consul 1885-1889 or Oliver H. Simons, Consul 1889-1893.

38 The *Martha Davis* was built in 1873 and operated services between China and Boston.

it quite time that something is done for them. Under the present regime in our colonies, if a man runs away from his ship, or fails to leave in the one selected for him, he is cast out of the Sailors' Home to beg, be imprisoned – or die in the gutter – perhaps even deprived of the last few charitable offices extended by all nations and people to those who are passing "beyond the shadow."

A VISIT TO CANTON

As the reader may require a change of air after the last somewhat melancholy chapter, and as almost everybody who goes to China makes a point of visiting Canton, I propose making a trip there by the pleasantest route, that is by water.

At half past seven a.m., after a light breakfast of frog-curry – which is considered a delicacy out there – flavoured with excellent Penang chutney, we hurry off to the Praya to catch the eight o'clock boat.[39] If we missed that we should have to wait until 5 p.m., as only two (Canton) steamers leave Hongkong daily.

We soon catch sight of the Hongkong and Macao Steamship Company's swift boat.[40] It is a yellowish coloured American built vessel which looks like a floating

---

39 Hong Kong once had the Praya Central, a stretch of seafront that fell victim to reclamation in the late nineteenth century though the use of the term Praya (or sometimes Praia) to describe the waterfront continued until the Second World War and even beyond among older Hong Kong residents.

40 Halcombe means the Hongkong, Canton & Macao Steamboat Company (HCMSCo) founded in 1865.

three-storeyed house with numerous doors and windows reaching the entire length of the ship. Protruding above the upper deck is a huge crank somewhat resembling in shape a gigantic hand-pump.

A continuous stream of intending passengers passes up the gangway; and as we gain the crowded deck our nose is assailed by a variety of uncommon odours – uncommon I say because they are peculiarly "Celestial," or in other words confined to the people and places of the "Celestial Empire" – combining a selection of noisome scents distilled from hay-like tobacco, opium, unwashed humanity, garlic, dried seaweed, samshoo, fish and divers other commodities of daily life.[41] Each Chinese passenger carries a netted basket filled with old pots, pans, bowls, cups, remnants of the last meal and all manner of garbage – not forgetting a small stone or wooden pillow similar in shape and size to a brick. This article is always placed ready for immediate use; for directly John has completed his arrangements for the passage he spreads his mat on the deck and lies down, resting his neck upon this hard but serviceable pillow.[42]

---

41 Shamsoo, or alternatively samshu, is an alcoholic drink from China that is made from fermented rice and resembles sake.

42 "John" being slang for a Chinese person – see f/n 29.

A river scene

A village of boats, Canton

Entrance to a Yamen

Hong Kong seen from Kowloon

Interior of a temple, Canton

The Kwang Tap or Bare Pagoda, Canton

The Man-Mo Temple, Hongkong

A Chinaman never leaves anything behind him when changing his residence: only that which can be removed by hard scrubbing – not even a broken bottle or pot. He crams them in among his personal effects. Before leaving he actually lifts the dirty earthenware rice-pot off the stove, with a crust of burnt rice lining the inside, and carefully deposits it among his other goods and chattels.

Now the whistle sounds and the huge crank above us begins to move up and down. The paddles revolve and the vessel slowly leaves the wharf. Making our way to the upper-deck we pass out of the confusion and smell to quietude, cleanliness and fresh air. On the saloon deck we meet the skipper who is sure to be a jolly good fellow who insists upon our having a "whisky-and-soda" with him – or a "peg" which means the same or similar refreshment.[43]

The following extract, written many years ago, will give the reader a good idea of the scenery met with during a river journey to Canton.

"On leaving Hongkong the steamer threads its way through the shipping, presenting to the passengers a

---

43 A whisky-and-soda was invariably called a *stengah* in Shanghai and occasionally in Hong Kong. A "peg" is usually an undefined measure of any alcoholic drink poured in a glass. The terms "large (*badda*) peg" and "small (*chota*) peg" are equal to 60ml and 30ml, respectively, with "peg" alone simply referring to a 60ml peg.

capital panoramic view of the terraced city of Victoria, daily climbing higher up the sides of the Peak, until, shortly before reaching the extreme western limit of the Island, its course is directed towards the narrow channel, between the western end of the island of Lam Tao and a small islet, which gives access to the mouth of the Canton River.[44] The scenery at this point is well worth studying. The harbour of Hongkong, with its numerous beauties, and the broad expanse of isle-dotted sea beyond, are left astern, whilst the rocky shores of the narrow channel, upon which the only sign of life or population is perhaps a solitary fisherman hauling his curiously constructed lever-net to the bank, or the crew of a passing boat offering the sacrifice of lighted joss-paper to a tiny shrine erected on the jutting angle of the rock.

The short grasses covering the rugged surface of the granite glow at almost all seasons, with colours of peculiar richness, from a deep purple to tender yellow, forming a carpet the tints of which are interrupted here and there by boulders of fantastic form and ombre hue, or relieved by delicate groups of feathery bamboo, flourishing from some nook in which a few inches of soil have been formed

---

44 Lam Tao (or slightly later Lam-tao) = Lantau. Canton River is an alternative for Pearl River. It appears Halcombe is mistaken and the "small islet" – probably Ma Wan – is at the eastern end of Lantau rather than the western.

by the disintegration of the granite. A solitary hamlet, the only one visible in a distance of at least thirty miles, may be seen occupying the strand at the northern extremity of the island on the right hand. This absence of population along the shores of the river is due as much to the lawless nature of the people as to the barrenness of the soil. The villages which exist along the course of the river are for the most part planted at the head of secluded creeks and bays, where greater opportunities of defence against hostile attack or of withdrawal from the action of authority are presented. The deserted aspect of the shore becomes particularly noticeable as the steamer proceeds, coasting under the rugged cliffs which rise from the eastern bank, whilst on the left hand the channel rapidly expands into the broad estuary, the prospect being only bounded on the left hand by the rugged promontories of Lam-tao, which are usually shrouded in dense masses of rolling mist. As the steamer passes on, the island of Ling-ting is seen mid-channel, and is pointed out as the place of anchorage for the opium ships in days when traffic in the drug was contraband.[45] Large numbers of fishing boats dot the broad expanse, and at every shoal the stakes to which their nets are attached are seen protruding from the water. Three hours after leaving Hongkong, after accomplishing

45 Ling-ting being alternatively Lin Tin or Lintin Island and now Nei (or inner) Lingding Island.

a distance of about fifty miles, the Bogue is approached, the bay and the fort of Chuan-pe being first passed on the left hand.[46] The fortifications of A-hung-hoy Point are the first that attract attention, consisting in a long range of granite masonry pierced with embrasures for guns at the water level, with a wall running up the cliff in a semi-circle as a protection from attack in rear.[47] The shattered blocks of granite still lie as they were driven from their places by the guns of the British squadron in 1856.[48] Abreast of this fortification lie the North and South Wang-tong, or Bar-the-Way Islands, completely encircled with granite batteries, which, however are in no better

46 The Bogue, also known as Bocca Tigris, is now usually referred to as the Humen, the narrow strait that separates Shiziyang to the north and Lingding Island to the south near Humen (formerly Fumun) on the Pearl River estuary. Chuan-pe, or simply Chuanpe, Chuenpee or Chuanpi is an island in the Pearl River Delta known primarily for the Second Battle of Chuenpi in 1841 during the First Opium War that resulted in the Convention of Chuenpi, which was never ratified though laid the framework for the later Treaty of Nanking (1842), the first of the so-called "unequal treaties".

47 Anunghoy Island.

48 The Battle of the Bogue was fought between British and Chinese forces on 12-13 November 1856 during the Second Opium War. The British captured the forts in the Wangtong Islands on 12 November and the forts in Anunghoy Island the next day.

condition than those of the main. The defensive position is completed by the batteries of Tiger Island, lying a little further on, to the left hand is ascending. This island, a remarkable mass of rounded granite with precipitous sides, rising to a height of about 400 feet, takes its name from a resemblance, fancied by the Chinese, to a tiger's head. Europeans discover, on the contrary, a well-defined elephant's head and trunk formed by a declivity about the centre of the island. Others declare that, if it must be known by the name of some animal, it should be called *Bare* Island.[49]

Once inside the Bogue, the banks of the river become more cultivated with rice and sugar-cane. The steamer's course, which hitherto has been on the whole northly, is turned to the west shortly after passing on the right a range of hills surmounted by a prominent land mark known as the Second Bar Pagoda (from the existence at this point of shallows known as the Second Bar), and the masts of

---

49 And in part from the *Bocca Tigris* (see f/n 36) derived from the Portuguese *Boca do Tigre*, literally meaning "The Tiger Gate". Halcombe may not have seen the resemblance but the American Commodore Matthew Perry, who later played a leading role in the opening of Japan to Western trade, noted that: 'Although the resemblance is not at first very striking, it becomes quite obvious after examination.' It was a largely denuded island, hence Halcombe's Bare (Bear) Island joke.

the foreign shipping at Whampoa are shortly descried.[50] The scenery surrounding this anchorage, consisting of low, wooded hills, is extremely picturesque, but the aspect of the Chinese village, fitly denominated Bamboo Town, opposite which the steamer stops for a minute or two is repulsive beyond description. As the first view of purely Chinese habitations, the dilapidated and decaying tenements erected on piles along the shore usually inspire unmitigated disgust. Some amusement may be derived from watching the deft manner in which the boatmen and boatwomen of Whampoa manage their sampans, which crowd in a dense mass around the steamer, in the midst of a Babel of vociferations, and seem to escape by a daily miracle the peril of swamping beneath the still-revolving paddles."[51]

---

50 The pagoda being the Lotus (Lianhua) pagoda. Whampoa being romanised commonly now as Huangpu and Whampoa Island as Pazhou Island.

51 Halcombe does not stipulate where this long extract came from – merely from 'many years ago'. Indeed, 30 years previously as it appears to have been extracted from *The Treaty Ports of China and Japan: A Complete Guide to the Open Ports of Those Countries, Together with Peking, Yedo, Hongkong and Macao* by Wm Fred. Myers, NB Denys and Chas. King, (London and Hongkong: Trübner and Co./Shortrede and Co., 1867), pp.125-127.

For wealth, magnificence and naturally advantageous position, Canton – or more correctly speaking Kwang-chow-foo – may be classed among the most famous cities in the "Middle Kingdom," and, owing to its commercial relations and many attractions in the way of temples, pagodas and curios, the most noted among other nations.

This far-famed emporium stands on the northern bank of the Chen Kiang or Pearl River, in the province of Kwangtung – hence its designation among foreigners, the word Canton being a corruption of the name of the province by the earliest Portuguese and English residents; and is situated at Lat 23° 7' 10" N and Long 113° 14' 30" East, being bound on the north by the provinces of Hunan, Kwang-si and Kiang-si, on the north by Fuhkien and on the east and south by the sea.[52]

In consequence of its favoured position the traffic of other countries was directed to it at a very early period; and as far back as the tenth century after Christ it was regarded as one of the principal centres of commerce in the Far East. At that time the Arabian navigators traded between there and the ports of Western Asia; and to this day there exist several monumental relics of their time in the shape of Muslim structures and followers of

52 Kwangtung = Guangdong; Kwang-si = Guangxi; Kiang-si = Jiangxi; Fuhkien (more commonly Fukien) = Fujian.

Mahommed. One of the most notable of the former is the Mohammedan Mosque and Minaret – known to the Chinese as the Kwang T'ap or Bare Pagoda which was built by the early Arabian traders in A.D. 850, and stands in the Tartar quarter of the city, a little to the southward of the crumbling Tah Yah or "Flowery Pagoda."[53]

The mosque is a plain and simple structure consisting of a large hall, the roof of which is supported by ordinary Chinese pillars; while the white-washed walls are only relieved from their severe simplicity by a few texts from the Koran. The floor is of stone covered with matting; and the only article of furniture is a rude altar upon which stands a tablet inscribed with an invocation to the great "Lord-of-Ten-Thousand-Times-Ten-Thousand-Years."

The origin of the mosque is denoted by the shape of the arches that form two sides of the structure, close to

---

53 The Mahommedan Mosque and Minaret was built (probably) around A.D. 627 by Sa'd ibn Abi Waqqas. It is a mixture of Chinese and Arabic architecture. The minaret (tower referred to as the pagoda) has an Arabic inscription over the Chinese-style entrance and has been partially rebuilt a number of times. It is now known as the Huaisheng Mosque, or colloquially the Lighthouse Mosque. The Buddhist Flowery Pagoda is part of the Temple of Six Banyan Trees and was built around 1097. It was rebuilt in 1373 after a fire and then restored in 1900. The Tartar Quarter approximates roughly to what is now Guangzhou's Yuexiu District. It was traditionally the central base of the military in the city.

which stands a circular tower or minaret which rises to a height of 130 feet, gradually decreasing in diameter until the first story is reached, from where the tower takes a much smaller calibre. Some bushes and a tree have grown out of the platform of the first story which used to be reached by a spiral staircase in the interior, but owing to its ruinous condition the entrance was blocked up some forty years ago.

In the sixteenth century the Portuguese, who were the pioneers of European commerce in the Far East, found their way to Canton, the navigator Fernas Peres de Andrade being the first to arrive there.[54] They were followed a century later by the Dutch who in turn were succeeded and supplanted by the English who, in the seventeenth century, opened commercial transactions with the Chinese Close Corporation, organised for that purpose – our trade being conducted by the East India Company whose agents had already traded further up the

---

54 Fernão Pires de Andrade (DOB: unknown; Died: 1552) – Portuguese merchant, pharmacist, and diplomat employed by Afonso de Albuquerque, 1st Duke of Goa. Halcombe is incorrect – both Jorge Álvares (who is usually credited as the first European to reach China by sea during the Portuguese Age of Discovery), and Rafael Perestrello, reached China before Andrade in 1513 and 1516 respectively. Andrade arrived in 1517, though he was the first to make formal representations to the Ming.

coast at Amoy and in the adjacent island of Formosa.[55] A factory was established at Canton, and commercial transactions were carried on with remarkable success, and to the entire satisfaction of both parties, for a period of one hundred and fifty years: thus establishing the basis of our influence in the empire.

Tea was rapidly imported into England, and in the year 1689 a duty of five shillings per pound was for the first time levied on it by His Majesty's Customs. The celebrated Canton silks and other valuable products of this hitherto little-known empire speedily found their way into our market.

As we near Canton the sign which attracts our attention is the ever-moving panorama of ships, junks and sampans in endless variety – large trading junks with their high gaudily-embellished sterns, low bows and huge mat sails, and clumsy looking house-boats, with movable bamboo hoods, which make trips inland to Fatshan, being able through their light draft to ascend shallow channels and creeks where no other craft could go.[56] Darting about here, there and everywhere are the small shoe-shaped sampans

---

55 Strangely Halcombe is the only writer I can find who uses the term 'Chinese Close Corporation'. Presumably he means the merchants' guilds in Canton allowed to trade with foreigners. Amoy = Xiamen; Formosa = Taiwan.

56 Fatshan = Foshan.

conveying passengers. These boats and many others are sculled by coquettish young damsels whose shrill voices can be heard from afar as they glide laughingly along, ever ready with a joke or a pert reply.

Further on and near the shore are the celebrated "flower-boats" which are hired by wealthy merchants and mandarins for evening banquets and parties. On these occasions the boats are decked with vari-coloured transparent lanterns, made of paper and glass, flags and pennants; while deeply-rouged damsels sing songs of love and chivalry in a high falsetto voice to the accompaniment of silken-stringed lutes, gongs and other unmelodious instruments.

A large percentage of the enormous population live and die on the river. From infancy, male and female alike, they are taught to manipulate the *yuhloa* and oar, while the mother and father attend to domestic affairs or look to the sails.[57] These boat-people are an independent and thrifty set who live on a little rice, fish and vegetable flavoured with common white samshoo: the entire cost of an adult's board for one month not often exceeding two dollars. In the Canton River there are regular floating villages solely composed of hundreds of boats moored head and stern in long lines, so as to allow room for the

57 Halcombe means a *yuloh*, a long stern sculling oar.

traffic.[58] And there hundreds of people live happily – except when a *typhoon* happens to come that way. Then there is much wailing and drowning. But the "big-wind" does not often come; and when it does the missing ones are not noticed much in that ever-increasing multitude. Still further up the busy river and beyond the Shameen, where the European residents reside, is the far-famed Puntinqua garden, several acres in extent, which is well worth visiting.[59] Here may be seen the wonders of landscape gardening for which the Chinese are justly celebrated – miniature lakes half-hidden by water-lilies, and spanned by quaint and fantastic bridges, shady groves and winding paths embowered in flowery foliage, dwarfed trees of every description, terraces and creeper-covered pavilions and artist rock-work with here and there a small three-storied pagoda or lilliputian temple.

58 The Canton River being an alternative name for the Pearl River or Yuejiang.

59 Shameen, or now more commonly Shamian, is a sandbank island. Shameen literally means "sandy surface" in Chinese. The territory was divided into two concessions given to France and Britain by the Qing government in the nineteenth century. Shameen was connected to the mainland by two bridges: the British arch bridge, also called the "Bridge of England" built in 1861, and the French bridge to the east. Puntinqua Garden is sometimes referred to as Puntinqua's Garden and often described by European visitors as a "pleasure garden".

The fragrant *mak-li* of Jasmine flowers, planted around a little joss-house on an artificial island in the lake diffuse their fragrant perfume, pleasing the senses while the eye is enchanted by the quiet and sylph-like scene.

Here we may rest and think at leisure, letting our imagination run riot among the wonders which here abound. Looking back over a vista of years, we picture to ourselves the merchant prince of a bygone day wandering among the silent splendour of these archaic haunts with some favoured "barbarian" from the far-away land in the "Great Western Sea." I imagine them in those days, when a halo of mystery surrounded these distant shores, sitting together in yonder crumbling but romantic summer-house sipping a cup of the much-prized *cha* (tea) while the host, with an eye to business, expatiated even eloquently upon the virtues of that soothing beverage.

As in most other Chinese cities, the streets of Canton are built to exclude the fierce rays of a tropical sun and are seldom more than twelve feet in breadth, while the numerous stalls and protruding shop-counters tend to make them still narrower – hence the nauseating odours which assail our fastidious noses as we pick our way carefully about these narrow and slippery thoroughfares where filth and garbage are distributed freely and seldom cleared away, except by the force of nature. Lean wolfish-looking "wonks" or low-caste dogs hail our approach with howls of disapproval followed by sundry snarls and snaps which are anything but reassuring, being somewhat suggestive of hydrophobia.[60]

The streets are crowded with all sort and conditions of men; and no order or regularity is observed among them – half-naked coolies bearing handsome green-covered chairs of high officials, and shabby ones – the former often preceded by a retinue of rag-bedizened Yamen runners, soldiers and loafers – working coolies scantily covered and bearing heavy loads on either end of a bamboo which is balanced on the shoulder; respectable citizens sauntering along with enviable imperturbation, seemingly indifferent to sounds and odours, constantly fanning themselves; hawkers with their wares, making a great noise which no one takes any notice of; and last but by no means least, the inevitable beggars, many of them lepers.[61] These mendicants seem bent on annoying everyone and anyone indiscriminately and levying tribute from the entire population. A batch of these surly rogues march into a shop and stand wailing and moaning in front of the counter. No one thinks of driving them out; and at length the shopkeeper mildly expostulates by throwing

---

60 By which Halcombe means rabies.

61 A Yamen being the administrative office or residence of a local bureaucrat or mandarin.

them a few copper cash. Then they curse his illiberality and visit his neighbour.

Large signboards are suspended outside the shops where all manner of curios may be bought at a reasonable price. You must always by word, look, and gesture depreciate the goods you desire to purchase; and when the seller states his price you must laugh him to scorn and offer him one quarter of the amount asked. He will then slowly and systematically, for time is no object, beat the price back to half. Then you split the difference. He will smile nonchalantly, shrug his shoulders and say "No can". You shrug yours, say "maskee" and walk away – don't look back, though.[62] He won't let you go far before you hear his voice; and as you reluctantly return he will some again and say "Can do, one dolla."[63] Then give him ninety cents and go your way. You will be satisfied and will look so. So will he be satisfied and have reason to be – he won't show it.

Among the sights of Canton, the temples take a prominent place and are very interesting. The most noteworthy of them is the Temple of the "Five Hundred Gods" – called by the Chinese Fan Lum Sze – which is situated in the western suburbs and consists of a number of stately halls where a variety of enthroned deities, five

62 "Maskee" – China Coast Pidgin for "never mind".

63 "Dolla" = dollar.

hundred of them, preside in all the gilded pomp and magnificence befitting these satirical effigies of the great Buddhist worthies and religious fanatics of historical and mythological renown.[64]

While passing through the seemingly lifeless streets of the Tartar Quarter we come to the handsome Bell Temple or Temple of the Five Genii.[65] This institution, being well endowed, and also supported by considerable subscriptions among the Tartar military officials, is kept in better order than most of the temples within the city. After traversing the usual quadrangle in front, a flight of steps is reached, above which a highly ornamental gateway was built in 1842 from funds contributed by the celebrated Ki-ying, the Imperial Commissioner for foreign affairs.[66] In addition to the main hall containing an image of the Supreme Divinity of the Taoist faith,

---

64 The Hualin Temple, also known as the Temple of the Five Hundred Genii.

65 More commonly known now as the Temple of the Five Immortals, constructed in approximately AD 1377. Shortly after the installation of the temple's 3-metre-high, 5-ton bell in 1378, there was a plague outbreak in the city. Considered unlucky ever afterward, the "Forbidden Bell" has not been rung since.

66 Alternatively Keying or Qiying (1787-1858). He conducted several of the "unequal" treaties with the Western powers, including the 1842 Treaty of Nanking after the First Opium War and then the negotiations in 1858 after the Second

there are lateral enclosures each containing separate places of worship. The principal "sights" connected with this Temple were until lately its gigantic bell, and the stone images of five (supernatural) rams, but these latter were destroyed in a conflagration which consumed the rear building in which they stood some three years since. The legend with reference to the foundation of this Temple is that, some twenty centuries ago, five shepherds were seen on the site where the building now stands, who suddenly became transformed into an equal number of rams, while these again instantly changed into stone, a voice being heard at the same time proclaiming that, so long as these supernatural objects should be worshipped on this spot, the prosperity of the adjoining city should endure. From that day forward (runs the story) these images have remained on the identical spot, and it is certain that from time immemorial they have been looked upon with superstitious reverence; nor is it the less remarkable that the destruction of their shrine coincide so closely with the actual decline in the prosperity of the city. The stones were almost shapeless blocks of granite, about eighteen inches high and the same in length with some rude attempt at sculpture in the form of a ram's head. From them and their attendant legend Canton derived its soubriquet

---

Opium War. The settlement was repudiated by the Xianfeng Emperor and Ki-ying committed suicide.

of the City of Rams, but the legend itself is traced by Chinese philosophers to an accidental resemblance between the word signifying "ram" or "sheep" and the ancient designation of the province of Kwangtung. This is a striking corroboration of Professor Müller's dictum that all myths are merely amplifications of some forgotten sound.[67]

Immediately in front of the building in which these mystic stones were preserved stands a remarkable pile of masonry traversed by an archway some 20 feet in height and open at the crown in the centre, above which, from lofty rafters supported by pillars placed on the top of the archway, hangs an enormous bell. This was cast and placed in its present position, it is believed, some two centuries ago, but in consequence of a prophecy which was uttered at the time, foretelling calamity to Canton whenever this bell should give forth sound, it was deprived of a clapper and all means of access to it were removed. The knowledge of this prophecy served to bring about its fulfilment. When the bombardment of the defences of Canton took place in 1857, prior to the capture of the city, it was suggested to the commander of one of HM's ships to aim a shot at this bell, and the result was that,

67 Friedrich Max Müller (1823-1900), a British philologist and Orientalist of German origin. Credited with the creation of Indian Studies in Britain.

while calamity was indeed befalling the haughty city, the bell, struck by a cannon-ball, boomed forth its unwonted sound.[68] The effects of the shot are seen in the fracture of the lower rim of the bell. Immediately beneath it is placed a large iron censer, in which incense, offered to the spirit of the bell, is kept constantly burning.

On the east of the main hall is a small enclosure surrounding a pond, on the red sandstone floor of which is seen the shape of a gigantic foot, declared by the priests to be the impress left by the divine Buddha; and on the opposite side down a flight of steps is the shrine of Golden Flowers, where the deity who corresponds in China to the Venus Genitrix of Rome is besought to bless mothers with offspring. Images of the hand-maidens of this benign goddess are placed in shrines on both sides of the temple, each holding one or more newly born infants upon her knee. Mothers making vows or prayers before a particular image are accustomed to tie a piece of red cord around the figure of one of the infants in token of their wish. At the head of the enclosure is placed a small building containing an image of the mighty Kwan, the God of War. His frowning visage, and bow and sword suspended by the altar indicates the martial character of

68 During the Second Opium War. "HM" being Her Majesty as in the HMS designation of Royal Navy vessels.

the idol.[69] Here the Tartar aspirants for promotion make sacrifice before appearing at the examinations.

From an architectural point of view the official residences are well worth visiting. But it is not easy to gain admission to a Yamen – unless the great man is absent. Then by a judiciously bestowed "cumshaw" his underlings or runners will show you round.[70] These residencies are easily distinguished by their high triple gateways outside of which numerous proclamations and orders are posted up. On entering, the visitor passes several courtyards the sides of which are lined with the servants' apartments and treasury. But we have no time for more sightseeing now; we must hurry down to the landing-stage or we shall lose the Hongkong boat.

69 Kwan = Guanyu, alternatively Kwan Kung, the Chinese god of war but also around China a god of wealth and many other things.

70 Cumshaw = "grateful thanks" in the dialect of Xiamen – a China Coast pidgin word for a tip or financial inducement.

MAN-MO TEMPLE, AND PROCESSION

At the western end of Hollywood Road, in Hongkong, and on the left-hand side, stands a temple called the Man-mo which was originally – at least, before the occupation of the island – a shrine where poor fishermen and travellers in that locality used to pay their respects and make their humble offerings to the God of the Fishermen and other deities there.[71]

It had latterly fallen into a ruinous state, and in the middle of 1893 a subscription was made amongst the native population of the colony to effect repairs, rebuild a portion of this fane, and add an extra sanctuary to it.[72] The money having been liberally supplied for this purpose,* the work was commenced, and was completed for the China New Year in 1894. The old temple now looked really imposing – its interior resplendent with huge brass vessels, incense brasiers, giant candlesticks, all highly polished, banners, scrolls and other ecclesiastical

---

71 Man Mo Temple, 124-126 Hollywood Road, originally built 1847.

72 Fane being another word for a temple or shrine.

ornaments; and the exterior magnificently and tastefully embellished with square-shaped panels of artistically-moulded scenes comprising animals, mountains, lakes, bridges, temples and palaces, all done in plaster and afterwards carefully painted over with specially prepared pigments, which resist the action of wind and weather for ages. The roof was covered with quaint and elaborate designs after the same style but on a much larger scale.

> *As is customary, each subscriber received a round paper lantern which he burned for three nights outside his shop or residence to propitiate the Gods who are supposed to reward his generosity when they see his receipt-light.

In celebration of this important event in the history of the temple, and to propitiate and congratulate its deities, another large fund was raised among the Chinese for the purpose of having a grand pageant and erecting a reception-house for the mighty Sky Dragon who would come down to see the improvements made in the temple.

Great preparations went forward, and a magnificent spectacle was eagerly anticipated – thousands of sight-seers crowding into the colony from Canton and all parts of the surrounding country.

Outside the temple piles of long poles and bamboos of all sizes and lengths were brought – the former being fantastically painted in various bright-hued designs. With these a lofty scaffolding was soon raised to a height of one hundred or more feet, as the Chinese are particularly dexterous and rapid in this work. When this gigantic though fragile looking framework was complete, huge chests full of light mat-work panels, ornamented with effectively painted designs, appeared on the scene. These were soon emptied and the contents taken aloft and fitted, each into its proper place, forming a complete and gorgeous covering and lining for the framework – thus transforming it into a fairy-like fane of enormous dimensions from the roof of which flower-decked crystal chandeliers and silken-tasselled lamps of all sizes and descriptions, and highly embellished clock-work models with moving figures, were suspended. Round the walls of the interior costly scrolls, some of great antiquity and value, pictures by native painters and autograph verses and proverbs by famed poets, philosophers and dignitaries, were hung in artistic profusion.

In the centre and at the corners of the enclosure were ornamental stands for the musicians, around which were placed cages with bright-plumaged birds and pots of choice flowers and plants – many containing complete miniature trees, curiously stunted, and other cultivated freaks of nature.

At the beginning of the first moon, in our February, festivities commenced in earnest. A splendid procession, costing thousands of dollars, was formed. It was fully a mile in length and passed through every thoroughfare in the colony. First came the musicians headed by an enormous drum, beating cymbals and gongs and playing flutes, trumpets and other instruments too numerous and noisy to mention; then came hundreds of standard and screen bearers with vari-coloured silken banners, followed by gorgeously apparelled boys bearing arms and trophies. After these came fantastic stands with artificial trees upon whose branches were fixed young and beautiful girls in silk and satin-spangled robes to represent heroines of history and romance. Behind these little "Celestial" demoiselles came the younger sons of Han, also exquisitely dressed, carrying spears and bows and mounted on gaily-caparisoned ponies which were led by male attendants clad in red cloth and bunting. Following these were miniature temples with clockwork figures, the former being made with remarkable skill and ornamented with the highly-prized plumage of the kingfisher. Behind these came miniature "flower boats" each with its complement of enchanting damsels; and in their rear came huge monsters – animals with moving jaws and wagging tails, pursued by a number of half-human monstrosities with animal and reptile heads of great size, accompanied by boisterous clowns and lithesome acrobats who pleased the public greatly.

Following these were more musicians, models, figures, soldiers and standard-bearers; and finally the "Sky Dragon" himself appeared in all its pomp and splendour – with jaws distended and glaring red eyeballs rolling in a fierce and truly hideous manner about their wide sockets. This monster was constructed with wonderful ingenuity – its scaly body, nearly two hundred yards in length, and five feet in breadth, was made with silver paper; and on either side the forms of the numerous bearers were partially hidden by folds of yellow bunting, only their legs being visible as they carried it along, from time to time being relieved by relays of strong coolies.

Onward went the gigantic monster, its side-bells ringing and its myriad of legs scuffling along, to the intense delight of the spectators upon whose closely-packed heads one could have easily walked for miles, so dense was the crowd.

In front of the advancing dragon, danced two energetic harlequins carrying long ball-mounted poles with which they were supposed to direct the movements of this unearthly prodigy whose immense horned head moved impetuously from side to side in a most diabolical manner which must have impressed the awe-inspired spectators with its power and majesty; for they followed its every movement with staring eyes and gaping mouths. It was a sight they would never forget and might never see again.

In D'Aguilar Street some thrifty housewife had hung her washing out of a front window to dry; and as the procession advanced towards the house a great cry of rage and indignation was raised. The vast concourse came to a standstill and every eye was angrily fixed upon those fluttering clothes aloft there. They were a dastardly insult to the dignity and power of the mighty Sky Dragon and those accompanying it, and an omen of bad luck; and the procession could and would not proceed until they had been removed.

The poor guilty woman was nearly frightened out of her senses and wept bitterly that she should have thoughtlessly offended so great a deity. It is needless to say that her washing was soon taken in, and the procession moved on its course – the dragon's legs seeming to move all the merrier for the short rest.

The poor country folk were simply wonderstruck – they had never beheld or even imagined anything so grand and beautiful before; and would remember it to the end of their days. But the greatest surprise of all had been prepared for the evening. On the newly reclaimed spare ground facing the harbour, another lofty scaffolding had been raised, and this was covered from head to foot with every conceivable kind of firework. A spacious stand had been prepared for His Excellency the Governor, Sir William Robinson and Lady Robinson, and the chief English and Chinese officials.[73]

Early in the evening a steady stream of people began to pour from every quarter of the city, and by eight o'clock there were upwards of two hundred thousand people assembled there – lining the broad bund and its approaches, from east to west, and appropriating every inch of the reclamation ground. It was a dark night, and fortunately continued so.

At 9 p.m. the fireworks were lighted – rockets soared, hissing upward, forming arbours in the sky, while others shot up between them dispersing their brilliant fire-flowers far above; and catherine wheels revolved like golden watermills, showering their glittering spray around and

---

73 William Robinson (1836-1912), initially a specialist in the West Indies colonies, was appointed Governor of Hong Kong in 1891, serving to 1898 after which he retired. Lady Robinson was his second wife, Felicia Ida Helen Rattray. Lady Robinson died shortly after the events Halcombe describes and is buried in the Hong Kong Cemetery. Robinson is one of the few former governors of Hong Kong without a street named after him (the others being Young and Patten). Robinson Road in Mid-Levels is named after an earlier governor, Hercules Robinson (who served between 1859 and 1865).

dazzling the enchanted eye. Then a great, deep, trembling murmur of intense wonder and admiration arose above the loud-sounding music and musketry. From seaward there now came a fleet of fairy-like boats. One mass of gorgeous, quivering light, from innumerable lanterns, drifted nearer and nearer; and the soft music of many lutes came shoreward over the water, making merry company.

The wondering crowd had hardly got accustomed to this new sight, when the deafening din of gongs, bells and timbrels again attracted every eye to the eastward whence there came a multitude of sea-monsters, making a grand display. Fishes of every size and description were there, from a whale to a tiny sprat: all moving naturally along in a line which seemed to have no end. They were all lighted up inside, being made of transparent oiled paper, and really had a remarkably lifelike appearance and excited universal admiration from Chinese and European alike. Behind these came the old dragon which was also illuminated from head to tail; and the whole procession took more than an hour to pass a certain point.

All in that mighty multitude of spectators seemed remarkably quiet and well behaved and much merriment prevailed. For three or four days the procession moved about, gradually dwindling in length and grandeur until it was no more. Then the well-pleased people, after paying a farewell visit to the Man-Mo temple to make their little thank-offerings and view the alterations, dispersed to their respective homes for an enjoyable outing.

THE GREAT PLAGUE OF HONGKONG

During the latter part of April 1894, we heard in Hongkong that a strange and dreadful disease had broken out in Canton, whose inhabitants suddenly became panic-stricken and fled to Hongkong in thousands – every steamer arriving from there being crowded each trip, until the colony was densely packed with them. Then the startling news was spread abroad that the death-dealing pestilence – in all respects analogous to the Great Plague of London in 1665 and 66 – was in our midst.

At first, however, it was merely a rumour, then it was confirmed by the announcement that a couple of deaths had occurred from plague in Taipinshan, situated in the west end of the city. But very little notice was taken of, or credence given to these reports and no measures were taken to prevent the epidemic from spreading or to stop the inrush of natives from the affected districts. They continued to pour into the doomed colony which was just beginning to feel the oppressive warmth of a tropical summer. The foreigners resident there resented and ridiculed the idea of an epidemic invading or seriously endangering Hongkong – or even finding a sure foot-hold there. And, in spite of repeated warnings from more than one lip and more than one pen, for some time a sense of security and immunity from all danger was felt. This was altogether unjustifiable and fatal – as was soon amply demonstrated by Death in its most awful form.

The hidden depths of disgraceful insanitation were about to be revealed when too late to rectify or avert the resulting calamity and sacrifice – the human sacrifice imposed by the accumulated filth of many money-making years, during which time the lower classes of Chinese householders must have been treated by the Sanitary Inspectors with somewhat remarkable deference, leading to culpable neglect.

As is generally the case, when the tide of this hitherto wealthy colony was, financially and socially, at its lowest ebb, there was a freshet – a freshet of pestilence, which carried death, destruction and disgrace with its foul overwhelming tide.[74] All the world now held aloof, and wondered.

During the notable epidemic, known as the "Black Death" of 1348 and 49 which – originating in Asia, and sweeping westward to the countries of Europe, laid its decimating scourge upon London – we read that two

74 A freshet being the flood of a river from heavy rain or melted snow.

hundred persons were buried in the Charterhouse daily.[75] Even at that period, compare the population and area of London with those of Hongkong, and then imagine the hold which this dire disease must have had upon the colony, when over a hundred deaths from it occurred daily – until so many victims awaited internment that the dead could hardly be disposed of.

It was in every respect similar to the plague alluded to in eloquent language by Boccaccio in his introduction to the "Decameron" – and his description of it will give the reader a far better and more correct idea of what it was like in Hongkong and of its ravages, than anything I could write.[76]

---

75 Charterhouse Square lies on the edge of the City of London. With the existing London cemeteries unable to cope with the dead from the Great Plague, Sir Walter Manny, knight and friend of King Edward III, rented a section of land – just outside the City of London – as a burial site for plague deaths. It is thought that there could be as many as 10,000 bodies under the square.

76 Referring to the 14th-century Italian author Giovanni Boccaccio (1313-1375). The book contains 100 tales told by a group of seven young women and three young men as they shelter in a secluded villa just outside Florence in order to escape the Black Death afflicting the city. Boccaccio probably conceived of the Decameron after the epidemic of 1348 and completed it by 1353.

For some little time the infectious disease was confined to the western end of the colony; and, when too late, a cordon of British soldiers was drawn across Taipingshan to prevent the contagion spreading; and hopes were entertained that, with the first good shower of rain – as there had been a long period of drought – it would entirely disappear. The rain came and went, but the plague remained. It doggedly dodged from one street to another, silently, surely and fatally, creeping along in every direction, north, south, east and west. Then it met at the corners – and finally encompassed the whole colony; locking it and its terrified inhabitants up in a cold grasp of sudden death from which there seemed no escape, as the ships no longer came from there and all trade had ceased. Everyone expected death, and sat awaiting it – and it came.

A poor lean rat would creep out on the floor before you, and overcome with the disease, stagger and fall; then drag itself a little further away from its untenable hole, a little nearer you, as if for company, and die almost at your feet. That poor little thing was the first harbinger of death – a sure sign that the pestilence was stealing into your house; and you could not shut it out. Who would be the first? That was the awful question; and you all gathered together, and watched one another, looking for the first dreaded symptoms – a slight feeling of dizziness and faintness.

As this pestilence gradually gained way, the streets began to grow lonely, the shops were closed and blinds drawn down; and anon the sound of mourning was heard. At last only a few nervous and affrighted people darted here and there, or a corpse was carried out of a house. Perhaps a mangy dog, picking about the garbage in the gutters, suddenly started instinctively back as it came upon one of its kind wreathing about in spasmodic convulsions, jerking its poor head against the kerbstone, and foaming at the mouth which was snapping in the last agonies of a ghastly death that frightened the other sacred creature, which scampered away down the deserted street, running from death that was at work on either side.

Those who were able to, fled from the colony before it was too late and those who could not, went to their homes. Servants left their places and hurried off to join their families before death dispersed them. Two of my own servants went home and died: and several rats came out in my rooms all of which died from the plague – I buried them at once and took every precaution, burning sulphur and sandalwood continually, and plenty of carbolic acid and chloride of lime. But my wife and I fully expected every moment to be stricken with it, as I had marked symptoms and was very ill with a large boil for some time.

But in the midst of all this misery, desolation and death, some few heroic men worked and toiled for suffering humanity. The people of Hongkong – Europeans and Chinese alike – will never forget and may well be proud of the noble Christian men who fearlessly and faithfully tended the sick and comforted and assisted the grieved and afflicted during that great crisis. I am speaking of Doctors Cantile and Lowson both of whom attended daily at the bedsides of plague-stricken natives.[77]

Dr. Cantile was absent on a holiday, at Pekin, when the epidemic broke out, but he at once hurried back directly he heard of it.[78] Many a day have I met him hurrying

---

77 Dr James Lowson (1866-1935). A Scottish doctor, Lowson was just 28 during the Hong Kong epidemic though he held the post of Surgeon and Acting Superintendent of the Government Civil Hospital in Sai Ying Pun in Western District. He had graduated from Edinburgh University in 1888, and soon after left for Hong Kong.

78 Dr James Cantlie (1851-1926) was a Scottish doctor, and pioneer of First Aid, who worked at the Charing Cross Hospital, London, until 1888 when he moved to Hong Kong to establish the Hong Kong College of Medicine for Chinese (now the Li Ka Shing Faculty of Medicine, HKUMed). While there, one of his pupils was Sun Yat-sen. Cantlie was praised for his work on leprosy, tropical diseases and the response to the 1894 outbreak of bubonic plague in the colony. He returned

along through the death-haunted streets, fearlessly going into the worst places and houses – into the most filthy dens of disease, where the pestilence was raging with dreadful potency – to tend poor penniless people from whom he would take no fee, whom he helped out of his own purse and provided with medicines. If ever a man deserved to receive the honour of a knighthood, he does. Very few know the extent of his noble and high-minded magnanimity and unselfishness, and I take this opportunity of expressing my sincere appreciation and regard for his chivalrous and heroic conduct in befriending and saving the lives of hundreds of poor friendless people. I trust that this may be the means of bringing the exemplary conduct of these two gentlemen fully before the attention of the high authorities; as so many worthy but unassuming heroes got unwittingly passed by.

Our English soldiers there also acted splendidly throughout: and went through some dangerous and

---

to London in 1896 in poor health. However, he remained a public figure not least for his campaign that same year to win the release of Sun, kidnapped and held at the Chinese Legation by the Qing Dynasty. A plaque to Sun remains on Cantlie's final home at Cottered in Hertfordshire, where Sun recuperated after his ordeal. Cantlie remained active up until the First World War advising the military of operating front-line ambulance services.

fulsome work.[79] Many Chinese hid the bodies of their deceased relatives away in houses so as to avoid the premises being cleaned and disinfected. In consequence search parties had to be organized to enter every house, and hundreds of corpses were found secreted in this manner and were buried. Great piles of refuse and garbage were cleaned out from some houses, that must have taken years to collect, where the germs of disease were cultivated. And the soldiers came forward and volunteered to clean the city out, when no one else would venture even near or in the vicinity of a plague-stricken house. One noble young British officer, whose name I am ashamed to say I have forgotten, fell a victim to the plague – sacrificing his promising life for the sake of the colony: he died after a hard day's work with his men.

At first these poor fellows suffered terribly from heat, thirst and fatigue; and several being stricken with the disease, I wrote the following letter which appeared in the columns of the *Hongkong Daily Press.*

79 The soldiers were from the Shropshire Light Infantry then stationed in Hong Kong.

TOMMY ATKINS AND SANITARY WORK. TO THE EDITOR OF THE "DAILY PRESS"[80]

Sir – I do not altogether consider it right and expedient that our European soldiers in Hongkong should be allowed to further expose themselves to the plague, especially since one of them has already caught this terrible disease, by carrying out the sanitary operations – removing dirt, furniture, and even dead bodies with their own hands. The work would be equally well done if it were merely superintended by a European, the manual labour being performed by hired coolies, or even by the Indian rather than the European soldiers. It is not difficult to imagine how volunteers are required for certain work; those who will volunteer must step three paces to the front – or something of that sort. The consequence is that the men do not like to hang back, as they naturally enough suppose that those who do will be "marked men." Once can picture the company drawn up facing the officers. Volunteers are called for. For a few minutes ominous silence prevails. The sergeant

80 Tommy Atkins (or more often just Tommy) is slang for a common soldier in the British Army.

feels very uncomfortable; he looks at his comrades and steps forward; they follow like men and true Britishers whatever the odds may be. But this is not right and fair, nor is it wise and expedient. There is an advertisement in the papers for volunteers. It is very doubtful whether they are to be had for the glory of the thing. But there are plenty of able men (men I have seen and spoken to) who would undertake the sanitary work at once if they were moderately well paid for the trouble and risk. – I am, sir, yours faithfully.

C.J.H.H.

Hongkong, 30th May, 1894

P.S. – three more unfortunate soldiers have been attacked with dangerous symptoms, and there is no wonder that such is the sad case when we consider the scandalous treatment these unfortunate men are evidently subjected to. Those who are selected for this special sanitary duty are marched out of the barracks before 7 a.m., after a frugal meal, and on their arrival at the Tung Wah Hospital receive orders for the day.[81] No conveyance is provided for them. The poor fellows are advised

---

81 Constructed from 1870 and opened in 1872 on Po Yan Street, Sheung Wan, as the first hospital for the general public.

to smoke tobacco and take a little stimulant; but none is provided for them. They are left to work like slaves and gasp for some stimulant to help them through their arduous and unhealthy duties. I am not writing this from imagination; I have made enquiries from a gentleman working with them and have myself seen the men at work. No wonder that the poor fellows look so pale, fagged out, and miserable. All the refreshment that is provided at the hospitable Tung Wah headquarters is a large bottle of water. It is a crying shame that these hard-working helpless men, who are heroically exposing their lives for the benefit of the community, should be treated in this manner.

C.J.H.H.

After this the men were more hospitably treated by the community in general and were also better and more appropriately equipped and provided for against the dangers and hardships they heroically encountered while performing these exceptionally obnoxious though, be it said to their credit, self-imposed duties.

*

The symptoms of this fatal bubonic disease were exactly similar to those described by the ancient writers, Guy de Chauliac, Gentilis of Folingo and others, being manifested by a feeling of faintness, sometimes accompanied by blood-spitting, and always with high fever which remained throughout; then glandular swellings, which were very tender, came generally under the armpit or in the groin. After death the body turned black, decomposition setting in at once. But in very virulent cases I have seen men suddenly struck down in the street. The victim would stagger, like a drunken man, and fall – gasping for breath, and foaming at the mouth; and would frequently die before the hospital could be reached.

As all the hospitals soon became overcrowded with plague patients, mat-sheds had to be erected for their reception and treatment. At last, however, after thousands had been swept away, the colony began to shake itself free.[82] Slowly and surely the dire pestilence was driven

---

82 The 1894 Hong Kong plague, part of the third plague pandemic across most of Asia, was harshest in 1894, though returned annually between 1895 and 1929, killing over 20,000 people in total, with a fatality rate of more than 93 per cent. In 1894 admissions to hospital averaged 80 a day, and death peaked at over 100 per day. The areas most affected were the more overcrowded and included Taipingshan, Sai Ying Pun, Shek Tong Tsui and Kennedy Town as well as the area then known as Bowrington (between Wanchai and Causeway Bay).

away, being met and courageously grappled with by the army of young English military volunteers who gallantly rose to the occasion and, acting the part of scavengers and heroes, routed out and burned tons and tons of filth and rubbish which had been accumulating for years. After the subtle poison in the air had sufficiently expended itself and was not further impregnated with exhalations from the putrid ground and the dirt-heaps covering it – hot-beds where the atomic germs had developed and multiplied – the epidemic began to abate. And by the month of August the colony and its inhabitants once more assumed its wonted appearance. But they had learned a lesson from experience which will not easily be forgotten.

APPENDIX

Charles JH Halcombe's poetry

Charles Halcombe was a keen amateur poet and included some of his poetry in *The Mystic Flowery Land*. Several are reprinted here below…

Ode to Chefoo[83]
(written aboard the SS *Haeting*, July 4, 1888)

Now as I gaze upon thy peaceful strand,
By fragrant airs of early summer fann'd,
Ling'ring I watch each twilight shade pourtray[84]
The homely picture of a happy day
That now declines: but each receding scene
Will form the landscape of some future dream
Of perfect rest: and mem'ry will alight
On verdant ways, now fading, as the night

83 Yantai.

84 An archaic form of the word 'portray'.

Steals gently forward, and the soft-toned breeze
Trips lightly homeward o'er the Eastern seas.

Farewell to Amoy[85]
(written aboard the SS *Hailoong*, December 5, 1890)

Farewell, Amoy! In sadness I depart,
For 'mid thy rocks responses still my heart.
My fleeting hours upon your tranquil shore
Will be remember'd till my days are o'er,
With mem'ries dear.

Farewell, sequester'd nooks and sunny scenes,
Remembrance for a moment intervenes,
And touching Then and Now with kindly rays,
Fast setting in the sky of bygone days,
Brings peace to mind.

Farewell, snug harbour, with your old-world ships,
And antiquated sailors, from whose lips
Strange drowsy chaunts I've heard at morn and eve,
When, hoisting sail, the junks prepared to leave
With fav'ring tide.

85 Xiamen.

Farewell, half-hidden homesteads grandly graced
By Nature's fairest foliage interlaced;
Where weary eyes and hearts, find happy ease,
Beneath huge boulders and o'erhanging trees
Near to the sea.

Farewell, majestic highlands, where the crown
Of dying Day reclines upon a gown
Of unseen flowers, lone groves of wind-swept firs,
And quaint, time-hallowed sepulchres,
Watched o'er by Death.

Grim sentry! Keep your silent watch, until
Above the rugged crest of yonder hill,
Far eastwards, in the early morning skies.
The everlasting Star of Life shall rise
To give you rest.

Great Death! My wondering mind doth often rest
Upon your silent home, and in the west
Can picture you alone, in calm survey
Of countless ages, looking far way,
Whence Life shall come.

Farewell to Formosa[86]

(written aboard the SS *Formosa*, November 25, 1891)

Farewell Formosa! Isle of crystal springs,
And fabled hills of gold;
O, for the countless treasures absence brings –
The mem'ries that you hold –
All left untold.

Farewell, Tamsui! Little seaside town[87]
Beneath the banyan trees,
Whose foliage weaves an emerald gown
Of beauty – but disease
Lurks in its folds.

Farewell, lone hill! Whose sylvan slopes are paved
With ling'ring smiles of day;
And long-forgotten names are still engraved
On pages by the way –
Where pass the clouds.

Farewell, Red Fort!! No longer form those towers

86 Taiwan.

87 Tamsui, alternatively Danshui, is the seaside district of Taipei, adjacent to the Tamsui River and overlooking the Taiwan Strait.

The exiled sentries keep
Their lonely vigil thro' the anxious hours,
While exiled comrades sleep,
In armour clad.[88]

Kozinga's warlike junks no longer rise
Above the sea's dark line;[89]
No more beneath the gold of evening skies
Their blood-stained weapons shine –
For they have gone.

Gone! But a crumbling relic of their age
Is watching grimly o'er
The changing scenery of the time-worn stage,
Whose actors are no more –
No more than dust.

88 Halcombe is referring to the Santo Domingo Fort in Tamsui, originally built in 1628 by the Spanish. The Dutch rebuilt the site in 1644. The fort was leased by the British as a consulate from 1868 until 1972 (with several years' break during World War Two). It is now a tourist attraction.

89 More commonly Koxinga (1624-1662), Southern Ming general who defeated the Dutch in Taiwan and established a dynasty which ruled part of the island from 1661 to 1683.

Also available in the *China Revisited* series:

WANDERINGS IN CHINA
Hong Kong & Canton
Christmas & New Year 1878/1879
BY CONSTANCE GORDON-CUMMING
Introduced & Annotated by
PAUL FRENCH
CHINA REVISITED

LING-NAM
Hong Kong, Canton &
Hainan Island in the 1880s
BY BENJAMIN COUCH "BC" HENRY
Introduced & Annotated by
PAUL FRENCH
CHINA REVISITED

ROVING THROUGH SOUTHERN CHINA
An American's Explorations of Hong Kong, Macao and Canton in the early 1920s
BY HARRY A FRANCK
Introduced & Annotated by
PAUL FRENCH
CHINA REVISITED